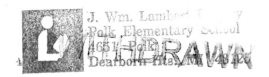

D1717027

Let's Take a Trip
An Ancient Forest

by Guy J. Spencer

photography by Frank Staub

Troll Associates

Library of Congress Cataloging in Publication Data

Spencer, Guy.
    An ancient forest.

    (Let's take a trip)
    Summary: Follows a group of visitors as they explore
and enjoy Redwood National Park in California.
    1. Redwood—Juvenile literature. 2. Forests and
forestry—California—Juvenile literature. 3. Forests
and forestry—Oregon—Juvenile literature.
4. Redwood National Park (Calif.)—Juvenile literature.
[1. Redwood National Park (Calif.). 2. National parks
and reserves. 3. Forests and forestry—California]
I. Staub, Frank J., ill. II. Title. III. Series.
SD397.R3S97   1988   634.9'758   87-3487
ISBN 0-8167-1167-4 (lib. bdg.)
ISBN 0-8167-1168-2 (pbk.)

The author and publisher wish to thank the Redwood Region Conservation Council for their generous assistance
and cooperation.

Millions of years ago, when dinosaurs roamed the earth, redwoods towered over the land. As the land slowly changed, the dinosaur died out. But the redwood has survived! How has this hardy tree been able to survive the changes on the earth? Let's take a trip to the coast redwood forest and find out.

The coast redwoods are found along the Pacific coast of California and Oregon. In this northwestern part of the United States, rain is plentiful. The redwoods thrive on the foggy climate that dampens the air and the ground.

Its broad but shallow root system allows the redwood to drink lots of water. The trunk of the tree can hold as much as 8,000 gallons at once! Water flows from the roots, through the trunk and the branches, to the leaves, or *needles,* of the tree. Sunlight causes green chlorophyll in the needles to make food from the water and air. This nourishment helps the tree to grow.

The thick sturdy bark is another reason the redwood has survived. It keeps out insects and fights the diseases that can kill or destroy other trees. The redwood's bark is twelve inches thick with a texture that does not easily burn.

But look closely at any tree in the forest, and you will probably see a burn mark. Fire and lightning are natural enemies of redwoods and other trees. Some scars are so deep that caves have been formed at the bases of the trees. But wildfires are rare in the redwood forest because it is so damp.

The *Immortal Tree* has been struck by lightning and flooded up to the fish mark! Long ago, a woodsman even tried to chop it down! But the Immortal Tree is still alive and over 900 years old.

Often the redwood tree is damaged when another tree falls on top of it. But the redwood is able to heal itself. It forms a funny-shaped knot, or *burl*, right on the damaged spot. Burls are prized for their beautiful grains. They are often used to make table tops, wall hangings, and clocks.

Sometimes large areas of the forest are cut down by companies who want trees for timber. This is called *clear-cutting*. Clear-cutting usually happens in the parts of the forest owned by the timber companies. Later the companies plant new little trees in place of the ones that were felled. Cutting down sick or damaged trees is called *selective cutting*. It is the main kind of cutting done in state and national parks.

Only a certain number of redwoods are
allowed to be cut down each year. George
sharpens the teeth on his chain saw. He is an
expert logger. To tell which way the tree will
fall, he looks at the way it is leaning. Then he
checks the wind conditions for the direction in
which it is blowing.

First, George cuts a notch in the tree from the side on which it will fall. Next, he makes a back-cut on the other side of the tree. Then, George pushes a wedge of wood into the back-cut to tip the tree forward.

"Timber!" cries George, as the tree begins to crash to the ground. George measures the tree and discovers that it was over one hundred feet tall! He cuts it into smaller sections, which will make it easier to move.

How old was the tree? By counting the rings, George can tell it was sixty years old. You can discover the age of any tree by counting the rings on its stump. Each ring usually counts for each year the tree has been alive.

Once the trees are cut, the movers take over in the logging area. Many of the logs are lying on steep slopes or deep in gulches. Cables and pulleys help bring the logs from these places to the trucks.

Loaders lift the heavy logs. Sometimes, it takes two loaders to lift one heavy log onto a truck. When a truck is full, the driver takes it over the rough terrain to a sawmill.

At the sawmill, logs are fed into a *debarking area*. Here, jets of water strip off the bark. The peeled logs are cut into twenty-foot lengths by a circular saw. Then they are cut into boards, which are usually an inch or two in thickness.

After being dried, the wood is sorted and
stacked. It is then sent to supply companies
that sell the lumber to builders and furniture
manufacturers. The best will be used for
outdoor furniture and beautiful redwood
houses. People know that this durable wood
will last for many years.

Buildings made from redwood trees can be found in many different places. The trunks of the trees were used for the pillars of a theater. One of the oldest buildings in North America was built using redwood planks. And the Ripley's Believe-It-or-Not Museum was built from just one tree.

The large areas that were cleared for timber are cleaned up with controlled fires. Foresters light leftover branches and underbrush with torches. They are careful to clear the surrounding area so that the fire does not spread. The ashes enrich the ground for the new trees that will be planted.

Hundreds of new little trees, or *seedlings,* are grown in nurseries. Helicopters collect cones from the tops of trees. Inside the cones are the tiny seeds from which the seedlings grow.

The seeds are kept cold until it is time to plant them in the nursery. Fourteen days later, sprouts appear. When the seedlings are just about one year old, they are planted in the forest.

Deep in the forest, redwood trees reproduce on their own. Seeds drop from cones onto the crowded forest floor. The tiny trees that sprout from these seeds must compete for light and space. Only the strongest survive!

Little sprouts can also grow from a tree stump or the trunk of a fallen tree. This is known as *sprouting*.

An example of sprouting is the *Cathedral Tree*, which is really nine trees in all. The Cathedral Tree was formed from sprouts that grew around a tree stump. Natural reproduction and replanting ensure the redwood's survival.

State and national governments have also made sure that the trees will survive! In 1968 a part of the redwood forest was declared a national park. Now the land is protected by law to preserve its natural beauty: healthy trees may not be cut down; animals may not be hunted. Surrounding the Redwood National Park are state parks. State governments have also declared that the trees may not be felled.

The Ladybird Johnson Grove is in the Redwood National Park. In this grove people are able to wander among the tall trees. Birds, wildflowers, ferns, and bushes share the forest with the redwoods. You might even catch a glimpse of a hawk or a great horned owl.

Animal life on the forest floor offers more attractions to visitors. The redwood forest is home to many different kinds of animals. The Roosevelt elk, the black-tailed deer, squirrels,

rabbits, striped skunks, gray foxes, raccoons, and many more can be found on the forest floor. And keep your eyes open for a little toad, popping up from a deep pile of needles!

One of the great attractions in the Redwood
National Park is the tallest tree in the world.
It is taller than the Statue of Liberty and
nearly 600 years old!

Perhaps the most interesting of all the redwoods is the *Candelabra Drive-Thru Tree*. The tunnel through which many cars have passed is really a hollowed-out fire scar! Every year as the tree grows, the gap begins to close. It must be widened in order for carloads of tourists to pass through.

Today small redwoods stand side by side with their ancestors in the forest. Look closely and you'll see that life goes on, deep in the redwood forest.